E
MO
Moncure, Jane Belk

Word Bird's winter
words

DATE			
AG 14 '87	AG 19 '89	MY 13 '91	JUL 05 '95
AG 26 '87	ND 24 '89	JY 22 '91	DEC 16 '95
FE 8 '88	JA 31 '90	OC 15 '91	
MY 25 '88	FE 20 '90	OC 29 '91	AUG 08 '96
			NOV 16 '96
JE 29 '88	AP 12 '90	DE 10 '91	DEC 13 '96
DE 29 '88	JE 8 '90	DE 30 '91	FEB 04 '97
FE 11 '89	JY 17 '90	JY 13 '92	NOV 12 '97
MR 21 '89	JY 23 '90	OC 19 '92	DEC 26 '97
AP 8 '89	AG 7 '90	NO 3 '92	JAN 29 '98
JE 27 '89	OC 13 '90		SEP 10 '98
AG 3 '89	NO 12 '90	MAR 09 '95	NO 29 '01
			FE 15 '06
			FE 07 '14

© THE BAKER & TAYLOR CO.

WORD BIRD'S
WINTER WORDS

by Jane Belk Moncure
illustrated by Vera Gohman

THE
CHILD'S
WORLD

ELGIN, ILLINOIS 60120

Distributed by Childrens Press, 1224 West Van Buren Street, Chicago, Illinois 60607.

Library of Congress Cataloging in Publication Data

Moncure, Jane Belk.
  Word Bird's winter words.

  (Word house words for early birds)
  Summary: Word Bird puts words about winter in his word house—snow, mittens, sled, icicles, Santa Claus, and others.
    1. Vocabulary—Juvenile literature.   2. Winter—Juvenile literature.   [1. Vocabulary.   2. Winter.
3. Christmas]   I. Gohman, Vera Kennedy, 1922-   ill.
II. Title.   III. Series: Moncure, Jane Belk.   Word house words for early birds.
PE1449.M534   1985   428.1   85-5942
ISBN 0-89565-309-5

    2 3 4 5 6 7 8 9 10 11 12 R 91 90 89 88 87 86

WORD BIRD'S
WINTER WORDS

Word Bird made a ...

word house.

"I will put winter words
in my house," he said.

He put in these words –

snow

snowsuit

cap

scarf

mittens

snowboots

snowflakes

snowball

snowman

snow shovels

sled

skis

ice skates

icicles

19

log fire

jingle bells

cookies

wreath

Christmas tree

stockings

reindeer

Santa Claus

gifts

CHRISTMAS

surprises

Can you read these winter word

snow

snowball

snowsuit

snowman

cap

snow shovel

scarf

mittens

sled

snowboots

skis

snowflakes

ice skates

ith Word Bird ?

Christmas tree

icicles

stockings

log fire

reindeer

jingle bells

Santa Claus

cookies

gifts

wreath

surprises

31

You can make a winter word
house. You can put Word
Bird's words in your house
and read them too.